not a fa

THERE IS NO FORGIVENESS
WITHOUT REPENTANCE.

THERE IS NO SALVATION
WITHOUT SURRENDER.

THERE IS NO LIFE
WITHOUT DEATH.

THERE IS NO BELIEVING
WITHOUT FOLLOWING.

JOURNAL

Published in Louisville, Kentucky by City on a Hill Studio. City on a Hill Studio and Not a Fan are registered trademarks of City on a Hill Studio, LLC.

The publishers are grateful to Ross Brodfuehrer for his collaboration and writing skills in developing the content for this book.

Additional copies of this guide along with other not a fan study resources may be purchased online at **cityonahillstudio.com**

Scripture quotations are taken from the HOLY BIBLE: New International Version® Copyright © 1973, 1978, 1984 by International Bible Society. Used by permission of Zondervan Publishing House. All rights reserved.

ARE YOU A FOLLOWER OF JESUS?

I know. I know. You've been asked this question before. Because it's so familiar, there is a tendency to dismiss it. Not because it makes you uncomfortable. Not because it's especially convicting. The question is dismissed mostly because it doesn't feel necessary.

One of the most sobering passages of Scripture tells of a day when many who consider themselves to be followers of Jesus will be stunned to find out that He doesn't even recognize them. In the Gospel of Luke chapter 13, Jesus tells of a day where everyone who has ever lived will stand before God. On that day many who call themselves Christians and identify themselves as followers will stand confidently in front of Jesus only to hear him say, "I never knew you. Away from me." If you've just assumed you are a follower of Jesus, I pray that this video series produced by City on a Hill will either confirm that confidence or it will convict you to reevaluate your relationship with Jesus and bring you to a commitment to follow Him.

Kyle Idleman
Teaching Minister
Southeast Christian Church / Louisville, KY

ABOUT THIS LITTLE BOOK

When fans attend a game or a theatrical production, they often receive a program. A program basically tells you what others will do – who will play quarterback, who will perform the lead. A fan then observes, critiques, and applauds what these others do. Though a fan may, at times, find himself living vicariously through an on-field player or on-stage actor, in actuality the fan doesn't really do anything himself.

A fan receives a program. But what does someone receive when he comes not just to observe, but to get in the game, join the cast, enlist in the action? Players get playbooks. Actors get scripts. Soldiers get field manuals. Doers get instruction books.

And that is what this journal is intended to be - more of a field manual than a glossy program. Admittedly, some parts of this little book are "program" describing the characters and storyline portrayed in the drama. But more importantly, this journal is meant to help you discover your role on Christ's team, your storyline in God's grand production, your post among the fighting ranks.

More importantly than knowing your role as a follower is knowing the One you are following: to personally know your coach, your captain, your director. The best followers know intimately the one they are following. So more than anything else, we hope this Journal will do that: help you not just follow, but know and love the One you are following.

For the next six weeks of your Not a Fan experience, we are asking you to carry this Journal with you; to consult it each morning, noon and night for prompts, suggestions, thoughts, and encouragement. Its presence can remind you of your role as Follower rather than a mere Fan. Bring it each week to your group as well, to help you recognize and celebrate your development in the daily decision to be a **Completely Committed Follower of Jesus.**

not a fan.

WEEK ONE

FAN OR FOLLOWER?

FAN OR FOLLOWER?

WHAT STOOD OUT TO YOU FROM LESSON 1?

DAY 1

NOTE: Besides these suggestions, you can always go to the Not a Fan website, notafan.com, for further ideas and encouragement, or visit the not a fan Facebook page.

MORNING QUOTES

"Then he said to them all: "Whoever wants to be my disciple must deny themselves and take up their cross daily and follow me."

— Luke 9:23

"We say to Jesus, 'I don't mind you making some changes in my life,' but Jesus wants to turn your life upside down. We say, 'I don't mind a little touch-up work' but Jesus wants complete renovation. We're thinking tune-up, He's thinking overhaul. We think a little decorating, why not, but Jesus wants a compete remodel."

— Kyle, not a fan. Series

MORNING SUGGESTION

DTR: Define The Relationship. Take a few minutes in the space below to define your relationship with Jesus. What it is now? And what do you want it to be?

_____

_____

_____

_____

_____

_____

_____

NOON REMINDER

Try taking five minutes for prayer. Close your eyes and, in your mind, picture Jesus. Watch Him turn, look at you, and hear Him say, "If you would come after me, you must deny yourself, take up your cross, and follow me." Hear Him say these words again and again. Become aware of your reaction to His invitation.

AFTER THE FIVE MINUTES HAVE PASSED, JOT YOUR THOUGHTS BELOW.

Note: *Some of the suggestions, like this one, may sound a bit inane or even non-traditional. We encourage you to try each exercise with an open mind. Give it 100%. When someone takes golf lessons or martial arts training, the instructor often gives them exercises that feel awkward, uncomfortable or even irrelevant to their goal. The athlete who improves the most is usually the one who cooperates most with the training.*

EVENING REFLECTION

ASK JESUS TO REFLECT ON YOUR DAY. SAY TO HIM, "JESUS, TELL ME ABOUT MY DAY." WRITE WHATEVER STANDS OUT BELOW.

_____

_____

_____

_____

_____

_____

END OF THE DAY FOCUS

"No one can come to me unless the Father who sent me draws him..."

— John 6:44

Jesus has invited you – not just you in general, as part of the crowd, but you yourself, by name – to follow Him. Sleep with that thought of Jesus personally calling you at the forefront of your mind.

DAY 2

MORNING QUOTE

"Whenever I listen to you preach, I feel like you are trying to interfere with my life."

– Kyle Idleman, not a fan. Series

MORNING SUGGESTION

LOOK AHEAD TO WHAT YOU HAVE SCHEDULED TODAY. ARE YOU WILLING TO HAVE JESUS INTERFERE? WRITE YOUR RESPONSE BELOW.

HOW DO YOU FEEL ABOUT YOUR RESPONSE?

_____

_____

_____

_____

_____

_____

_____

NOON REMINDER

Try repeating this phrase aloud ten times, "Lord Jesus, come interfere in my life." (Again, this is one of the suggestions that may sound childish or impractical, but what do you have to lose by trying it?)

WHAT COMES OUT OF THIS EXERCISE FOR YOU?

_____

_____

_____

_____

_____

_____

_____

_____

_____

_____

EVENING REFLECTION

WHAT DID YOU LEARN TODAY ABOUT YOURSELF AND YOUR WILLINGNESS TO HAVE JESUS INTERFERE IN YOUR DAILY LIFE?

I LEARNED...

_____

_____

_____

_____

_____

_____

_____

_____

_____

_____

_____

END OF DAY THOUGHT

When it comes to Jesus interfering in your life, what would change in your spirit if you believed the following words:

"For I know the plans I have for you; plans to prosper you and not to harm you, plans to give you hope and a future."

– Jeremiah 29:11

Go to sleep with these words on your mind.

DAY 3

MORNING QUOTE

"Is Jesus one of many, or is He your one and only?"
— Kyle, not a fan. Series

MORNING SUGGESTION

Bring a favorite worship song or hymn to mind. Sing it aloud, even if softly. Write any words or phrases that stand out to you.

AFTER DOING SO, WRITE YOUR REACTION TO WHAT YOU HAVE DONE. LASTLY, NOTE YOUR SENSE OF JESUS' REACTION TO YOUR WORSHIP.

NOON REMINDER

When a person has a "one and only," he often writes love notes, even poetry, to the beloved.

BEFORE MOVING ON WITH YOUR DAY, WRITE A FEW WORDS TO JESUS TELLING HIM WHAT YOU THINK OF HIM.

EVENING REFLECTION

Whatever you are doing this evening, imagine doing it with Jesus.

WRITE ONE DIFFERENCE THAT WOULD MAKE TO YOU.

END OF DAY THOUGHT

"The Lord your God is with you,
the Mighty Warrior who saves.
He will take great delight in you;
in his love he will no longer rebuke you,
but will rejoice over you with singing."

— Zephaniah 3:17

You began the morning singing to Jesus. Singing to Him is fitting because He is worthy of your love. He is perfect love. As you go to sleep, imagine Him singing over you - a sweet song of His commitment, protection, forgiveness, and favor.

DAY 4

MORNING QUOTE

"In the same way, those of you who do not give up everything you have cannot be my disciples."

– Luke 14:33

MORNING SUGGESTION

WHO ARE YOU MOST TEMPTED TO PUT AHEAD OF AND TO LOVE MORE THAN JESUS?

TRY TO DESCRIBE WHY BELOW.

WHAT DID YOU GAIN FROM THIS EXERCISE?

NOON REMINDER

Think again of the person you named this morning, the one who is most likely to be in competition with Jesus for preeminence in your life. For a few minutes, try holding a mental image of Jesus alongside a mental image of the person who would be in greatest competition with Him. Simply become aware of what it is like when these two images are put side by side. As you do, compare the two below.

WHAT CAME FROM THIS EXERCISE?

EVENING REFLECTION

Imagine saying your evening prayers to the person you are most likely to put ahead of Jesus.

HOW WOULD THAT GO? HOW WOULD IT COMPARE TO PRAYING TO JESUS? EVALUATE THE DIFFERENCE.

END OF DAY THOUGHT

Read Colossians 1:15-18 and consider the supremacy and nature of Jesus Christ.

"The Son is the image of the invisible God, the firstborn over all creation. For in him all things were created: things in heaven and on earth, visible and invisible, whether thrones or powers or rulers or authorities; all things have been created through him and for him. He is before all things, and in him all things hold together. And he is the head of the body, the church; he is the beginning and the firstborn from among the dead, so that in everything he might have the supremacy."

— Colossians 1:15-18

DAY 5

MORNING QUOTE

"Is your relationship with Jesus moving from casual to committed?"

– Kyle Idleman, not a fan. Series

MORNING SUGGESTION

Try describing the difference you see between admiration and devotion.

ADMIRATION IS...

_____

_____

DEVOTION IS...

_____

_____

**WHICH DESCRIPTION LOOKS MOST LIKE YOUR RELATION-
SHIP TO JESUS?**

_____

_____

_____

_____

_____

_____

_____

**How would you distinguish the difference between
admiration and devotion? Share it with us using** #iamnotafan

**DECIDE IF YOU WILL ADMIRE JESUS OR DEVOTE YOURSELF
TO JESUS TODAY.**

_____

_____

_____

_____

_____

_____

NOON REMINDER

For a few minutes, close your eyes and imagine yourself wholly devoted to Christ. Picture yourself as a totally committed follower. How would that feel? What would you do? What would be different? Don't rush this. Take the time to focus. After the meditation, jot down your thoughts below.

_____

_____

_____

_____

_____

_____

_____

EVENING REFLECTION

Close your eyes and reflect on your day. As you do, confess sin, and immediately receive Jesus' forgiveness. Don't give the Evil One a foothold by holding on to your guilt.

Thank Jesus for the good things as you recall them, and imagine Him receiving your thanks. Notice anything from which you want to learn.

WRITE YOUR THOUGHTS BELOW.

_____

_____

_____

_____

_____

_____

END OF DAY THOUGHT

**IMAGINE JESUS PRAYING OVER YOU LIKE A PARENT WOULD
A CHILD. WHAT MIGHT HE SAY?**

_____

_____

_____

_____

_____

_____

DAY 6

MORNING QUOTES

"Would you please tell him that the Bible teaches moderation in all things? Would you please tell him that it doesn't have to be all or nothing?"

— Kyle Idleman, not a fan. Series

"I know your deeds, that you are neither cold nor hot. I wish you were either one or the other! So, because you are lukewarm—neither hot nor cold—I am about to spit you out of my mouth."

- Revelation 3:15-16

MORNING SUGGESTION

For something to be hot, it must be heated. To be cold, it must be cooled. If an object is lukewarm, then it is either being equally heated and cooled, or being neither heated nor cooled.

If you are to be hot, then you must be sufficiently heated. Every stimulus you allow in your life will either heat or cool your love for Jesus.

Today we want you to record your habits as you go through your routine. At the end of the day, we will look at which habits "heat" your passion for Jesus and which "cool" your walk with Him.

THE WAY I WAKE UP IS...

_____

_____

_____

_____

WHAT I DO FIRST IS...

_____

_____

_____

_____

MY MORNING ROUTINE IS...

_____

_____

_____

_____

MY FOOD, DRINK, TOBACCO, CAFFEINE, ALCOHOL AND DRUG CONSUMPTION IS...

WHAT IS MOST IMPORTANT TO ME IN THE MORNING IS...

WHAT MOST INFLUENCES MY MOOD IN THE MORNINGS IS...

WHILE I DRIVE/COMMUTE, I...

NOON REMINDER

Journal about your habits while at work or school.

MY ROUTINE AT WORK IS...

_____

_____

_____

WHEN I HAVE A CHANCE FOR A BREAK, I...

_____

_____

_____

THOSE I TALK TO THE MOST ARE...

_____

_____

_____

THE WAY I PROBLEM SOLVE IS...

_____

_____

MY FOOD, DRINK, TOBACCO, CAFFEINE, ALCOHOL AND DRUG CONSUMPTION IS...

FOR A PICK-ME-UP, I...

DURING MY COMMUTE HOME, I...

EVENING REFLECTION

Catalogue your typical evening pattern.

WHEN I GET HOME, THE FIRST THING I DO IS...

MY EXERCISE PRACTICE IS...

MY FOOD, DRINK, TOBACCO, CAFFEINE, ALCOHOL AND DRUG CONSUMPTION IS...

I SPEND MOST OF THE EVENING...

MY FAVORITE THING I NEVER MISS IS...

MY TV HABITS AND INTERNET USAGE ARE ...

THE WAY I SPEND MY WEEKENDS IS OFTEN...

_____

_____

**CIRCLE THE HABITS THAT WARM YOUR HEART FOR JESUS.
PUT A BOX AROUND THOSE THAT COOL YOUR INTEREST
IN HIM.**

Note: *We are not asking if a certain habit is sinful or not. This question
is about you and how these habits modify your spiritual temperature.*

WHAT DID YOU GAIN FROM THIS EXERCISE?

_____

_____

_____

_____

END OF DAY THOUGHT

Meditate on Revelation 3:15-16.

DAY 7

MORNING QUOTES

"From this time many of His disciples turned back and no longer followed Him."

– John 6:66

KEEP OUT - RESTRICTED AREA - AUTHORIZED PERSONNEL ONLY "Here's another question: Are there certain areas of your life labeled 'off limits,' or does Jesus have all access?"

– Kyle Idleman, not a fan. Series

MORNING SUGGESTION

Before leaving for the day, go for a walk and spend some time in prayer – asking yourself the question, "Is there anything in my life that I am keeping off limits to Jesus?"

WRITE WHAT YOU DISCOVER BELOW.

_____

_____

_____

_____

_____

NOON REMINDER

AGAIN, GO FOR A WALK AND SPEND SOME TIME IN PRAYER.
DID YOU SEE ANYTHING THAT IS OFF LIMITS TO HIM? IF SO,
WRITE IT BELOW.

_____

_____

_____

_____

_____

f **◻** **🐦** **Describe in 10 words or less what your heart felt as
you died to self. #IAMNOTAFAN.**

EVENING REFLECTION

"Death. That is really what it means to follow Jesus. We choose to die to ourselves and live for Him."

– Kyle Idleman, not a fan. Series

Try walking around your home, saying to Jesus, "I give you this, and this, and this..."

DESCRIBE BELOW WHAT THIS EXERCISE WAS LIKE FOR YOU.

END OF DAY THOUGHT

Before bed, try getting on your knees and saying to Jesus, "I surrender all."

not a fan.

WEEK TWO

FOLLOW ME

WEEK 2
FOLLOW ME

WHAT STOOD OUT TO YOU FROM LESSON 2?

_____

_____

_____

_____

_____

_____

_____

_____

_____

_____

Note: *As you begin your second week of using the journal, please know that you can use this journal in any way that helps you follow Jesus. You may want to write notes and revelations beyond those that are requested. Or you may want to adjust the questions or exercises to take them in a different direction you find more helpful. This is your journey, so let the Holy Spirit lead you in how to use this journal.*

DAY 1

MORNING QUOTE

"The Bible says in Romans that all of us have sinned and fallen short of the Glory of God. In other words, none of us are good enough. We've all said things we shouldn't have said. We've all done things we shouldn't have done. And so we scrub and scrub at the stain, but the stain just won't come out.

And we reach this point, where we're not sure what to do. And so we live in denial of the stain. Or we blame other people for the stain. Or we rationalize and justify the stain. Or we just live in guilt and fear hoping somehow that no one will notice."

— Kyle Idleman, not a fan. Series

MORNING SUGGESTION

Be honest. What is one of your biggest stains? What failure, sin, foolish mistake has left a huge mark on your life?

IF YOU ARE WILLING, DESCRIBE IT IN WRITING. IF YOU ARE NOT WILLING, TRY TO DESCRIBE WHY.

IN THE PAST, WHICH OF THE FOLLOWING HAVE YOU DONE WITH THIS STAIN?

☐ denied it   ☐ ignored it   ☐ blamed others for it

☐ rationalized it   ☐ justified it   ☐ lived in guilt over it

WHAT EFFECT HAVE THOSE WAYS OF DEALING WITH THE STAIN HAD ON YOUR LIFE?

NOON REMINDER

As painful as it may be, take a couple of minutes to think again about some of your biggest "spills" and their subsequent stains. What images come to mind? Try drawing what your stains might look like to Jesus. (Yes, it's another "silly" exercise, but try it and then notice the effect.)

f ⊙ 🐦 **What mistake do you have to ask forgiveness for? Share it with the Not a Fan community and declare today the first day you are set free from that mistake and commit to living without that weight. Include the hashtag** #iamnotafan

EVENING REFLECTION

As our life awareness grows, we recognize that there isn't just one stain on one couch, but all of our furniture is marred - every relationship, every effort, every day is stained in some way. What do you do with the awareness of not just a few stains, but the chronic spilling and staining in your life?

☐ hide it   ☐ fight it   ☐ medicate it

☐ minimize it   ☐ confess it   ☐ justify it

AS MY AWARENESS OF SIN GROWS, I...

_____

_____

_____

_____

_____

END OF DAY FOCUS

Meditate on what sleep is like for you when your sins are heavy on your mind. Then consider what your sleep is like when you are confident your sins are removed. Decide which mindset you want to have as you sleep.

DAY 2

MORNING QUOTE

"Matthew understood that to follow a Rabbi was a 24-hour-a-day commitment Matthew understood that it was not just knowing what Jesus knows, it was going to be living how Jesus lived. Matthew understood that in order to follow Jesus, he must call Jesus 'Lord.'"

— Kyle Idleman, not a fan. Series

MORNING SUGGESTION

Take a few moments to imagine your morning ahead. Anticipate situations that will likely occur. In each case, picture yourself following Jesus into that situation. For example, if you awaken your children, envision yourself walking into the bedroom behind Jesus, with Him going ahead of you and showing you what to do and how to do it. Or if you have a client meeting, imagine Jesus walking into that office ahead of you, and you following His lead on how to listen, speak and act.

AFTER TAKING A FEW MINUTES TO PICTURE YOUR MORNING FOLLOWING JESUS, JOT DOWN ANY THOUGHTS IN THE SPACE PROVIDED BELOW.

_____

_____

_____

_____

_____

_____

_____

_____

_____

_____

_____

_____

Tell us - we'd like to know! Using only 1 word, describe your intentions for today. Use #iamnotafan to share with the Not A Fan community.

NOON REMINDER

REMEMBER THIS MORNING'S EXERCISE? WHAT EFFECT DID IT HAVE ON YOUR MORNING?

Think about your afternoon ahead, again picturing Jesus going ahead of you, and you following Him.

NOTE BELOW ANYTHING YOU WANT TO REMEMBER.

EVENING REFLECTION

Review your day in your mind's eye. Notice any times you really did mentally follow Jesus into a situation, and allow Him to take the lead. What was it like? Also notice the times you simply forgot or weren't willing to let Him lead.

JOURNAL WHAT YOU SEE AS THE DIFFERENCE IN THE TWO WAYS OF ENTERING SITUATIONS.

IF FOLLOWING JESUS IS INDEED A 24-HOUR-A-DAY COMMITMENT, THEN WHAT WOULD IT LOOK LIKE TO FOLLOW JESUS AS YOU REST?

_____

_____

_____

_____

_____

_____

_____

_____

_____

_____

_____

_____

_____

_____

_____

❏ ⭕ 🐦 **How are you going to open up the spaces in your life to let the right things in? Use #iamnotafan to share with us so we can try, too!**

DAY 3

MORNING QUOTE

"Doulos is the Greek word for slave. A slave had no rights. A slave signed over everything to the master, even his own identity. A slave's one word job description was obey. So Matthew understood, to call Jesus Lord, was to call himself a slave."

– Kyle Idleman, not a fan. Series

MORNING SUGGESTION

Do you want to be radical in following Jesus? Make a list of your primary possessions – house, cars, bank accounts, etc. Then make a list of your skills – gardening, teaching, repairing, selling, nursing, etc. Add a list of your core identities - husband, coach, leader, mother, artist, etc. Then sign all these over to Jesus.

POSSESSIONS	SKILLS	IDENTITIES

If you're ready to move from fan to follower, make your commitment in writing below.

Lord Jesus, because You are the giver of the above, and because of Your sacrifice for me, Your free gifts of forgiveness and everlasting life and Your great and indescribable worth, I hereby relinquish my rights over all of the above to You and Your will.

Signed _____

Date _____

NOON REMINDER

As you look back on your morning, what was it like to live, or what would it have been like to have lived, those hours with all you have surrendered to Jesus?

LIVING SURRENDERED TO JESUS IS LIKE...

EVENING REFLECTION

Did you actually sign over the possessions, skills and identities of your life to Jesus this morning?

Whether you did or not, reflect on what it was like even thinking about signing over all your rights to Jesus. What effect does facing a decision to actually sign on the dotted line have on you?

END OF DAY REFLECTION

WHAT POSSESSION, SKILL OR IDENTITY IS MOST DIFFICULT FOR YOU TO SIGN OVER TO JESUS? WHY?

Go to sleep imagining either:
1. Laying this at Jesus's feet
2. Clutching this thing to your chest while telling Jesus "No"

DAY 4

MORNING QUOTE

"I meet people every week who are slaves to something, but they found freedom when they became a slave to Jesus Christ. They were slaves to possessions or slaves to their own pleasures, they were slaves to people, what other people thought of them. But they discovered that true freedom is only found when they live as a slave to Jesus Christ. Instead of shame and bondage and death, we find joy and grace and eternal life. You will never know true freedom until you have completely surrendered and become a slave to Jesus Christ."

– Kyle Idleman, not a fan. Series

MORNING SUGGESTION

A fish taken out of the water is a pitiful sight as it struggles and reels in the open air. For a fish, to be freed from the constraints of water is to struggle in an environment it was not created for.

THINK OF A PARTICULARLY TEMPTING SIN. WHEN YOU THROW YOURSELF INTO THAT SIN, WHAT RESULTS? TO WHAT DOES THAT LIFE INEVITABLY LEAD?

_____

_____

_____

_____

_____

_____

_____

_____

Determine whether or not living in that sin is indeed like being a fish out of water.

NOON REMINDER

Try saying the following out loud and noticing how you feel when you say each:
- I will be a slave to pleasure.
- I will be a slave to possessions.
- I will be a slave to what other people think.
- I will be a slave to money.
- I will be a slave to sex.
- I will be a slave to status.
- I will be a slave to my career.
- I will be a slave to my family.
- I will be a slave to Jesus.

WHAT IS YOUR REACTION TO THIS EXERCISE?

_____

_____

_____

_____

_____

_____

_____

Try to remember this image the next time you are excited by the prospect of giving yourself to this idol.

END OF DAY FOCUS

Read 1 Samuel 7:12. Samuel used a rock to remember God's help in the Israelite's time of need. Before bed, choose an object that will help you visually remember God's presence with you.

_____

_____

_____

_____

DAY 5

MORNING QUOTE

"She wants a divorce."
– Kyle Idleman, not a fan. Series

MORNING SUGGESTION

Like Eric in our drama, we've all had to say things we never thought we would have to say, such as she wants a divorce, or I am addicted, I am sorry I hit you, I had an abortion, I was fired, you are not my first lover, and so on.

THINK OF THE HARDEST THINGS YOU HAVE HAD TO SAY BECAUSE YOU WERE NOT FOLLOWING JESUS. THEY WILL BE PAINFUL TO WRITE, BUT THE PAIN OF RECALL CAN PROTECT YOU FROM THE PAIN OF REPEAT.

WHAT DO YOU NOT WANT TO HAVE TO SAY AT THE END OF THIS DAY?

_____

_____

_____

_____

_____

_____

_____

_____

NOON REMINDER

Consider the following words. Circle those that stand out to you today.

"If being a slave to sin has left you broken and bruised and you find your life is in pieces... my master loves you, and if you let Him, He'll take the pieces of your life and turn them into a beautiful mosaic. My master invites all who are weary *and heavy burdened to come to Him and find rest for your souls, because His yoke is easy and His burden is light. And when you became a slave to my master, He makes you His son."*

EVENING REFLECTION

If Christ makes a mosaic from our sin, what has He done with yours? Look over the difficult sentences you listed this morning. How could each be rewritten because of what Jesus has done for you?

For example, "She wants a divorce" could become, "I saw I was a jerk and learned to love her again" or "My divorce broke me open, and though we didn't get back together, I know now I have to lean on Jesus in everything I do."

IF CHRIST MAKES A MOSAIC FROM OUR SIN, WHAT HAS HE DONE WITH YOURS?

HOW COULD EACH BE REWRITTEN BECAUSE OF WHAT JESUS HAS DONE FOR YOU?

_____

_____

_____

_____

_____

END OF DAY FOCUS

What sentence do you want on your lips as you go to bed tonight?

_____

_____

_____

_____

_____

_____

_____

_____

_____

DAY 6

MORNING QUOTE

"When Jesus said to Matthew, 'Follow me,' He was making it clear His invitation to follow is not just for the religious elite, for the morally upright, or for those who have their lives together. His invitation is for all of us who are hiding stains.

Then he said to them all: "Whoever wants to be my disciple must deny themselves and take up their cross daily and follow me."

- Luke 9:23

'Anyone' is a pretty inclusive word. Anyone can follow Jesus. Anyone who ever thought to themselves, 'I've gone too far... my stains are too big...'.

Anyone who has ever lain awake at night and said 'I can't believe what I have done'. Anyone who has ever looked in the mirror and said to themselves, 'I can't believe what I have become.' Anyone can follow.

Anyone who knows down deep that they've got really nothing to offer Jesus. Really, it's what Jesus offers us that changes things. On the day He said to Matthew, 'Follow me,' something changed in him that day. And how do we know all this about Matthew's life? How do we know about his past failures and mistakes? Because he tells us."

— Kyle Idleman, not a fan. Series

MORNING SUGGESTION

READ THE MORNING QUOTE OUT LOUD, WHILE STANDING IN FRONT OF A MIRROR. NOTE YOUR REACTION.

NOON REMINDER

READ TODAY'S MORNING QUOTE AGAIN, SLOWLY. WRITE BELOW WHAT YOU THINK JESUS IS SAYING TO YOU THROUGH IT.

_____

_____

_____

_____

EVENING REFLECTION

Anyone who looks at themselves honestly knows they have nothing to offer God. It's what God offers us that changes things.

Complete this sentence as if Jesus were speaking to you:

"_____ (your name), I am offering you...

WRITE YOUR RESPONSE.

_____

_____

_____

_____

_____

END OF DAY FOCUS

Tell Jesus your response to His invitation again before you close your eyes in sleep.

DAY 7

MORNING QUOTE

"Morgan, you could never make a stain so big that it would keep us from loving you."

— Kyle Idleman, not a fan. Series

MORNING SUGGESTION

Try substituting your name in the sentence above. Say it aloud. Now imagine hearing Jesus say those words to you. Hear Him say it several times. Become aware of your inner response to these words.

WRITE YOUR RESPONSE BELOW.

_____

_____

_____

_____

_____

_____

_____

_____

_____

_____

IS THAT THE MINDSET IN WHICH YOU WANT TO LIVE OUT THIS DAY? WHY?

_____

_____

_____

_____

_____

NOON REMINDER

Sit, close your eyes, and hear Jesus speak the words, "You could never sin big enough to keep me from loving you." Imagine yourself fully accepting these words, agreeing with them, believing them.

IF YOU DID, WHAT EFFECT WOULD IT HAVE ON YOUR...
- **EMOTIONS**
- **CLOSEST RELATIONSHIPS**
- **OUTLOOK ON LIFE**
- **FEELING TOWARD JESUS**

_____

_____

_____

_____

_____

EVENING REFLECTION

"When Morgan trusted her parents' unconditional love was real, she not only admitted her stain, she bragged about it. Her stain came to represent her total acceptance."

— Kyle Idleman, not a fan. Series

Imagine absorbing the words, "_____, you could never make a stain big enough to keep me from loving you." Imagine those words soaking into the very fabric of your being the way the finger nail polish soaks into the white couch. Imagine these words becoming a "stain" on your soul that won't come out – in this case, a good stain, a permanent mark that the world can never scrub away.

END OF THE DAY FOCUS

"_____, you can never sin so much as to keep Jesus from loving you."

not a fan.

WEEK THREE

WHAT MUST I DO?

WEEK 3
WHAT MUST I DO?

Write your responses to the final questions of the group session here.

WHAT, IF ANYTHING, DO YOU THINK JESUS IS ASKING YOU TO GIVE UP THESE DAYS?

_____

_____

_____

_____

_____

HOW DO YOU DETERMINE THAT HE IS ASKING THIS OF YOU?

_____

_____

_____

_____

_____

WHAT DO YOU SEE YOURSELF DOING ABOUT IT?

_____

_____

_____

_____

_____

DAY 1

MORNING QUOTE

"On this trail called life, all of us are following someone's directions. None of us are really blazing our own trail. We all follow a path that's been laid out for us by someone claiming to know the way. The question is: whose directions are you following? What path are you on?"

– Kyle Idleman, not a fan. Series

MORNING SUGGESTION

Try this, even though it might sound childish: Draw a winding path and on it a stick figure that represents you. Then draw a large sign post. On the sign, name the path you are on. It might be called "Dad's Trail" if you have basically been following in your father's footsteps. Or it might be "Easy Lane" in view of the fact that you do whatever seems easiest. It could be "Wall Street" because for you it has been all about the money. Or it might be "Service Street" as you are truly striving to put others first. In any case, be honest. Name the road you are on.

TRY TO DESCRIBE IN THREE SENTENCES OR LESS WHY YOU HAVE CHOSEN THIS PATH.

NOON REMINDER

Look back over your morning, and the way you lived it.

WHOSE PATH DID YOU FOLLOW? WORKAHOLIC DRIVE? AVOIDANCE ALLEY? LOVER'S LANE? HOW DO YOU FEEL ABOUT THE PATH OF YOUR MORNING?

_____

_____

_____

_____

_____

Every moment is a fork in the road. You can stay on the current path or turn to a new way.

WOULD IT BE A GOOD IDEA TO STAY ON YOUR MORNING ROAD OR TAKE A NEW WAY? IF YOU WERE TO TAKE A NEW WAY, WHAT WOULD IT BE NAMED?

_____

_____

_____

_____

EVENING REFLECTION

IF YOU STAY WITH THE PATH YOU ARE CURRENTLY ON, WHERE WILL IT LEAD IN 10 YEARS?

_____

_____

_____

_____

_____

_____

_____

_____

END OF DAY FOCUS

Picture the destination of the path you are on as vividly as you can. Can you rest peacefully knowing that is where you are headed? If not, picture the place you want to end up. Go to sleep with that destination in mind.

DAY 2

MORNING QUOTE

"Ultimately, what separates a fan from a follower is commitment. Many consider themselves followers, but what happens when their commitment is tested?"

– Kyle Idleman, not a fan. Series

MORNING SUGGESTION

ASK THE HOLY SPIRIT TO BRING TO MIND A TIME RECENTLY WHEN YOUR COMMITMENT WAS TESTED - AND YOU PASSED THE TEST! DESCRIBE WHAT HAPPENED BELOW.

HOW DID IT FEEL RECALLING AND DESCRIBING A VICTORY LIKE THAT?

_____

_____

_____

_____

_____

_____

_____

_____

_____

_____

WHAT DID YOU LEARN FROM THIS EXERCISE OF RECALLING VICTORY?

_____

_____

NOON REMINDER

Were you tested this morning? Almost certainly you were, if even in a small way.

DESCRIBE THE TEST, HOWEVER MINOR OR SIGNIFICANT, AND WHAT YOU LEARNED FROM IT.

HOW DOES WRITING ABOUT THIS TEST AFFECT YOU?

EVENING REFLECTION

Think of someone whose commitment to Jesus you admire. If you were to write a personal note thanking them for their inspiration and dedication, what would it say?

WRITE PART OF IT BELOW. AFTER COMPLETING IT, DECIDE WHETHER OR NOT YOU MIGHT ACTUALLY SEND IT.

END OF DAY FOCUS

Before you go to sleep, say a prayer of thanks to God for the person that came to mind in the above question.

DAY 3

MORNING QUOTE

"Fans want to follow Jesus, but not in a way that interferes with their lives. According to some recent research I came across, sixty-five percent of American adults between the ages of 18 and 42, would agree with this statement: 'I have made a personal commitment to Jesus that is still important.' Now on the surface, that seems pretty good. Sixty-five percent is impressive, but according to that same research, these committed Christians lived a lifestyle that was quote 'Statistically equivalent to that of non-Christians.' So when asked about their activities from the previous 30 days, Christians were just as likely as non-Christians to have gambled, visited a pornographic website or taken something that didn't belong to them.

They were just as likely to have gotten drunk and been involved with physical abuse. They were just as likely to have lied and talked badly behind someone's back. See, they said they were committed, but they weren't completely committed. Fans try to compartmentalize their life."

– Kyle Idleman, not a fan. Series

MORNING REFLECTION

Circle your honest viewpoint.

Getting high is...	OK	not OK	it depends
Sex outside of marriage is...	OK	not OK	it depends
Lying to protect myself is...	OK	not OK	it depends
Getting back at someone I don't like is...	OK	not OK	it depends
Viewing porn occasionally is...	OK	not OK	it depends
Stealing from a greedy corporation is...	OK	not OK	it depends
Leaving my marriage if I'm unhappy is...	OK	not OK	it depends
Doing whatever feels good is...	OK	not OK	it depends

WOULD JESUS AGREE WITH YOUR RESPONSES?

_____

_____

_____

NOON REMINDER

When we do our own thing in spite of what Jesus has said about it, then we are acting like we know better than Jesus. Choose one area where you disagree with Jesus and try completing this sentence.

I KNOW BETTER THAN JESUS WHEN IT COMES TO _____ (AREA OF DISAGREEMENT) AND THE REASONS I BELIEVE I KNOW BETTER ARE...

_____

_____

_____

_____

_____

WHAT DO YOU SEE FROM THIS EXERCISE?

_____

_____

_____

_____

_____

EVENING REFLECTION

Think of a time in the past when you disagreed with Jesus over how to live your life, and you did it your way. Recount what you decided, why, and how it turned out.

WHAT I DECIDED:

_____

_____

_____

_____

_____

_____

_____

WHY:

_____

_____

_____

_____

_____

_____

HOW IT TURNED OUT:

_____

_____

_____

_____

_____

_____

_____

WHAT DOES ANSWERING THESE QUESTIONS SHOW YOU?

_____

_____

_____

_____

_____

_____

_____

_____

_____

END OF DAY FOCUS

"This is what the LORD says—your Redeemer, the Holy One of Israel: "I am the LORD your God, who teaches you what is best for you, who directs you in the way you should go. If only you had paid attention to my commands, your peace would have been like a river, your well-being like the waves of the sea."

— Isaiah 48:17-18

Which phrase stands out to you from this section of Scripture? Go to sleep repeating that phrase over and over in your mind.

DAY 4

MORNING QUOTE

"Jesus made it clear. There is no such thing as 'selective allegiance.' When we decide to follow Him, He calls for a complete commitment and total surrender."

– Kyle Idleman, not a fan. Series

PICTURE JESUS IN YOUR MIND STANDING BEFORE YOU, AND SAYING TO YOU, "WILL YOU FOLLOW ME TODAY?"

NOON REMINDER

This may sound like another crazy idea - but why not try it? Talk to Jesus about your day so far - your concerns, decisions, and hopes. If you are concerned others might see you talking to an empty chair, you might try holding a phone up to your ear or putting in your ear bud so they can conclude you are just on the phone (and, in a way, you are "on the phone").

EVENING REFLECTION

WHOSE ADVICE ARE YOU MOST LIKELY TO FOLLOW IN EACH AREA?

	PERSON'S NAME	JESUS
RELATIONSHIPS		
MONEY		
SEX		
CAREER		
PARENTING		

ARE THERE STRONGHOLDS TO EACH SOURCE THAT KEEP US FROM PLACING CHRIST AS MOST IMPORTANT?

WEEK THREE

DAY 5

MORNING QUOTE

C. S. Lewis in his book, "Mere Christianity", *summarizes the call of Jesus this way: "Give me all. I don't want so much of your time and so much of your money and so much of your work: I want you...No half-measures are any good. I don't want to cut off a branch here and a branch there. I want to have the whole tree down. I don't want to drill the tooth, or crown it, or stop it, but to have it out. Hand over the whole natural self, all the desires which you think are innocent, as well as the ones you think are wicked-the whole outfit."*

JOURNAL YOUR REACTION TO TODAY'S QUOTE.

_____

_____

_____

_____

_____

NOON REMINDER

Imagine giving over the next five minutes to Jesus, and keeping the rest of the day to yourself.

Next, imagine giving the whole rest of the day to Jesus.

WHICH OPTION WILL YOU CHOOSE, AND WHY?

f ⃝ 🐦 **Schedule time today to not be busy. Sit, be still and take in your surroundings. Use your senses to observe everything going on around you. Include** #iamnotafan **and share a photo or drawing of what this looks like. This will look different for everyone, but sharing will encourage others to try.**

EVENING REFLECTION

DESCRIBE YOUR FAVORITE PART OF THIS DAY.

_____

_____

_____

_____

_____

DESCRIBE YOUR LEAST FAVORITE PART OF THE DAY.

_____

_____

_____

_____

_____

WHAT DID YOU LEARN FROM ANSWERING THESE TWO QUESTIONS?

_____

_____

_____

_____

_____

END OF DAY FOCUS

Read the morning quote three more times. Go to sleep focusing on whatever thought is strongest.

"Give me all. I don't want so much of your time and so much of your money and so much of your work: I want you...No half-measures are any good. I don't want to cut off a branch here and a branch there. I want to have the whole tree down. I don't want to drill the tooth, or crown it, or stop it, but to have it out. Hand over the whole natural self, all the desires which you think are innocent, as well as the ones you think are wicked-the whole outfit."

- C.S. Lewis

DAY 6

MORNING QUOTE

"Fans want to follow Jesus closely enough to get all the benefits, but not so close that he calls them to sacrifice or surrender things that are important."

"If you're unsure if you're a fan or a follower, then ask yourself this: 'When was the last time my relationship with Jesus cost me something?'"

– Kyle Idleman, not a fan. Series

MORNING REFLECTION

ANSWER KYLE'S QUESTION - WHEN WAS THE LAST TIME YOUR RELATIONSHIP WITH JESUS COST YOU SOMETHING?

HOW DO YOU FEEL ABOUT THE COST?

[Facebook icon] [Instagram icon] [Twitter icon] Finish this sentence. "Saying yes to Jesus meant saying no to _____." Use #iamnotafan to share your response with the Not a Fan community.

NOON REMINDER

DID FOLLOWING JESUS COST YOU ANYTHING THIS MORNING, IF ONLY A LITTLE DISCOMFORT IN NOT GOSSIPING WHEN YOU FELT AN URGE TO OR LISTENING TO A NEEDY CO-WORKER WHEN YOU DIDN'T FEEL LIKE IT? DESCRIBE THE COST ON THE NEXT PAGE.

_____

_____

_____

_____

_____

_____

_____

 When have you had to give up and quit something? What did you learn? How would you want to share that with your loved ones? What can be gained from your experience? Use #iamnotafan in your response to share with the Not a Fan community.

EVENING REFLECTION

A Flexitarian is a word for a vegetarian that eats some meats (the ones that they really enjoy). They are committed...until it gets inconvenient. Similarly, some followers of Jesus try to walk with Him without being fully committed.

WERE YOU A FLEXITARIAN IN YOUR WALK WITH JESUS TODAY? IF SO, WHAT WAS THE "MEAT" YOU ALLOWED YOURSELF TO EAT? HOW DID YOU FEEL AFTER EATING THIS "MEAT"?

END OF DAY FOCUS

Everything costs something. Even the "easy way," the way of low commitment, has its price. Sleep all day and it will cost you your physical vitality. Procrastinate on a work project and it costs you frustration and anxiety later. The real question is: what do you end up getting for the cost you paid? Think of something you know Jesus is asking you to do that will cost you, but instead of focusing on the cost, go to sleep focusing on the end result, the final reward.

What do you do when you are blocked? Go for a run? Workout? Get outdoors? Clean house? How do YOU reset? Use #iamnotafan in your response to share with the Not a Fan community.

DAY 7

MORNING QUOTE

"... sell your possessions and give to the poor, and you will have treasure in heaven. Then come follow me."

— Matthew 19:21

"Do you see what Jesus does here? He says to the man, 'Here is the path you're on. Here are the directions you're following. But you can't follow two sets of directions, so sell your stuff and come follow me.' At some point or another, in one way or another, all of us will have such a test of commitment where our devotion will be determined and our allegiance will be exposed. Jesus will not share you. He won't share you any more than a wife will share her husband or a husband, his wife. He wants all of you."

— Kyle Idleman, not a fan. Series

MORNING SUGGESTION

Can you picture Jesus as jealous, wanting you but not wanting to share you with other "gods"? Put your name in the blank below, then close your eyes and hear Jesus saying these very words to you.

"_____, I want you. I am jealous for you. You are important to me. I don't want to see you used and hurt by others. I will not share you with the gods of this world."

---

f ⊙ 𝕏 What would you tell your 10-year-old self about money? Use #iamnotafan in your response to share with the Not A Fan community.

NOON REMINDER

The problem with the man in this story was not that he had lots of money. The problem was that money had him.

WHAT HAS "HAD" YOU SO FAR TODAY? DESCRIBE WHOEVER OR WHATEVER HAS "HAD" YOU IN THE SPACE PROVIDED.

_____

_____

_____

_____

_____

EVENING REFLECTION

Circle what stands out to you from the paragraphs below:

"Some of you know you can't find satisfaction in a box. You can't buy happiness off a rack or order it off the internet or drive it off a lot."

– Kyle Idleman, not a fan. Series

"They exchanged their glorious God for an image of a bull, which eats grass."

– Psalm 106:20

"That's just not a good trade. Have you exchanged the glory of God for a car that can really handle the corners? Have you exchanged the glory of God for a job that He hasn't called you to, but pays really well? Have you exchanged the glory of God for a house that has all the upgrades? These things are all fine and good, but we have turned good things into God things. Fans of Jesus hold back because they're afraid they will miss out. Followers of Jesus go all in and find that when they finally let go, they discover what they really wanted all along. I wonder what happened to the rich young ruler. He walked away sad, but that's all we know. I wonder if he went on to become a richer older ruler."

– Kyle Idleman, not a fan. Series

"²⁸ Then Peter spoke up, "We have left everything to follow you!"

²⁹ "Truly I tell you," Jesus replied, "no one who has left home or brothers or sisters or mother or father or children or fields for me and the gospel ³⁰ will fail to receive a hundred times as much in this present age: homes, brothers, sisters, mothers, children and fields—along with persecutions—and in the age to come eternal life."

— Mark 10:28-30

"No matter what following Jesus costs us in this life, in the end we won't see it as a sacrifice. Rather we will see it as a privilege and an honor."

— Kyle Idleman, not a fan. Series

---

f ⊙ 𝕐 What holds you back from talking about money? Share it and be vulnerable and then start to let it go. Use #iamnotafan and share with the Not a Fan community.

END OF DAY FOCUS

Enter sleep thinking of one phrase from the paragraphs you just read.

not a fan.

WEEK FOUR

BURY THE DEAD

WEEK FOUR

BURY THE DEAD

WHAT STOOD OUT TO YOU FROM LESSON 4?

DAY 1

MORNING QUOTE

"Sometimes, in an effort to get as many people as possible to follow Jesus, I have, with good intentions, made following Him sound as attractive and appealing as possible...I realized that I have been guilty of selling Jesus. And in emphasizing only the parts about Jesus that I thought people would like, and begging people to follow Him, I have unintentionally belittled Him...I'm sorry if I've ever cheapened Jesus or made it sound like we're doing Him a favor by choosing to follow."

– Kyle Idleman, not a fan. Series

MORNING SUGGESTION

WHY DO YOU FOLLOW JESUS?
LIST THE REASONS THAT COME TO MIND FIRST.

_____

_____

_____

DO YOU FIND YOUR REASONS FOR FOLLOWING JESUS HAVE MORE TO DO WITH...

[ ] what Jesus offers you – forgiveness, answered prayer, eternal life, etc.

[ ] what He is like – His flawless integrity, His bottomless love, His selfless sacrifice, etc.

---

[f] [o] [t] **What is one activity that makes you feel useful and alive? Use #iamnotafan and share with the Not a Fan community.**

NOON REMINDER

Take a few minutes to describe why Jesus is worthy to be followed.

JESUS, YOU ARE WORTHY FOR ME TO FOLLOW BECAUSE...

_____

_____

_____

_____

_____

_____

_____

_____

_____

_____

EVENING REFLECTION

"If you were interested in getting to know my daughter, you had better come with everything you got; or I'll send you packing."

- Kyle Idleman

DO YOU FIND YOURSELF INTERESTED IN KNOWING JESUS – NOT ONLY WHAT HE COMMANDS AND NOT JUST HIS WILL FOR YOUR LIFE – BUT HE HIMSELF, HIS VERY PERSON-HOOD?

☐ Yes, definitely!   ☐ Not sure, maybe?   ☐ No, not really.

TRY TO DESCRIBE WHY YOU ARE PASSIONATELY SEEKING TO KNOW HIM, DISPASSIONATELY SEEKING TO KNOW HIM, OR NOT SEEKING TO KNOW HIM AT ALL.

END OF DAY FOCUS

Bring to mind your mental picture of Jesus, how you see Him in your mind when you think of Him. Don't rush ahead to the words below. First realize how you see or sense Jesus when you think of Him.

Does this mental picture contain or portray the qualities you described today at noon? For example, if you said Jesus is full of love, is your mental representation of Jesus bursting with love? If not, add depth and color and weight to your mental picture of Jesus so that it aligns with your description. That is, make your mental image match what you believe that Jesus is really like. Go to sleep meditating on this more accurate mental representation of Jesus.

DAY 2

MORNING QUOTE

"As they were walking along the road, a man said to him, 'I will follow you wherever you go.' Jesus replied, 'Foxes have dens and birds have nests, but the Son of Man has no place to lay his head.'"

— Luke 9:57-58

MORNING SUGGESTION

Weigh this question in your mind.

WOULD YOU RATHER BE HOMELESS WITH JESUS OR HAVE A BEAUTIFUL HOME WITHOUT JESUS? JOURNAL YOUR THOUGHTS.

_____

_____

_____

_____

_____

NOON REMINDER

Focus on your mental image of Jesus from last night. Meditate on His glory, beauty, kindness. Imagine Him coming to you and saying, "I see you. I know you. I love you. I will never leave you."

After meditating in this way, see if you can honestly hum or sing the words to this old hymn:

I'd rather have Jesus than silver or gold;
I'd rather be His than have riches untold;
I'd rather have Jesus than houses or lands;
I'd rather be led by His nail-pierced hand
Than to be the king of a vast domain,
Or be held in sin's dread sway;
I'd rather have Jesus than anything
This world affords today.
I'd rather have Jesus than men's applause;
I'd rather be faithful to His dear cause;
I'd rather have Jesus than worldwide fame;
I'd rather be true to His holy name.

EVENING REFLECTION

AS YOU LOOK BACK ON YOUR DAY, WHAT DID YOU WANT?

_____

_____

_____

_____

_____

_____

_____

WHAT DID YOU GET TODAY?

_____

_____

_____

_____

_____

WHAT DO YOU THINK OF WHAT YOU WANTED AND WHAT YOU GOT?

_____

_____

_____

_____

_____

_____

END OF DAY FOCUS

Bring to mind your improved mental picture of Jesus. Make up your own words to the song, _I'd Rather Have Jesus_. You would rather have Jesus than what? Enter sleep constructing and humming those personal words to Him.

DAY 3

MORNING QUOTE

"Please make trails wider so we can hold hands while hiking."

"Please avoid building trails that go uphill."

"Please spray the area to get rid of the bugs and the spiders."

"A small deer broke into our camp and ate much of our food. Could we please be reimbursed?"

— Complaints registered at the Bridger Wilderness Area

EVEN THOUGH SOME OF THEM MIGHT SOUND SILLY, WHAT ARE YOUR HONEST COMPLAINTS ABOUT WHAT IT IS LIKE TO FOLLOW JESUS?

_____

_____

_____

_____

"And I don't care how you position it, carrying a cross just isn't comfortable."

– Kyle Idleman, not a fan. Series

Following Christ does not mean denying that the journey is hard.

CAN YOU ACCEPT THAT YOUR CHRISTIAN WALK WILL OFTEN BE NARROW, UPHILL, ROCKY AND SOMETIMES DANGEROUS? JOURNAL YOUR THOUGHTS.

_____

_____

_____

_____

_____

_____

_____

_____

NOON REMINDER

Bring to mind your mental impression of Jesus. If not already present, add nail scars to the image.

WHAT EFFECT DOES THAT ADDITION HAVE ON YOUR HEART?

EVENING REFLECTION

Bring to Jesus, in prayer, the complaints that you listed this morning regarding how hard it is to follow Him.

WHAT KIND OF RESPONSE TO YOUR COMPLAINTS DO YOU THINK YOU RECEIVE FROM HIM? DESCRIBE IT BELOW.

END OF DAY FOCUS

Bring to mind your mental image of Jesus again. If your image is not already filled with compassion, fill your representation of Jesus with compassion, as much compassion as there is in the universe. Then imagine bringing your complaints, along with your grief and troubles of the day, to Him.

WHAT IS IT LIKE?

DAY 4

MORNING QUOTE

"Jesus has many who love the kingdom of God, but few who bear a cross. He has many who desire His comfort, but few who desire His suffering. All want to rejoice with him, but few are willing to suffer for Him. He writes; there are many who admire his miracles, but there are few who follow in the humiliation of the cross."

— Thomas à Kempis

WHICH WORDS BELOW BEST DESCRIBES YOUR INTERNAL REACTION TO TODAY'S READING? OR, IF YOU PREFER, ADD YOUR OWN WORDS.

☐ shame   ☐ excitement   ☐ guilt   ☐ frustration

☐ anxiety   ☐ joy   ☐ boredom   ☐ fear   ☐ hope

☐ pride   ☐ determination

TRY TO DESCRIBE WHY THESE WORDS ARE YOUR REACTION TO THE READING.

_____

_____

_____

_____

NOON REMINDER

WHAT HAS BEEN YOUR PRIMARY EMOTION THIS MORNING?

☐ shame ☐ guilt ☐ excitement ☐ frustration

☐ anxiety ☐ joy ☐ fear ☐ boredom

☐ hope ☐ pride ☐ determination

TRY TO DESCRIBE WHY.

_____

_____

_____

_____

_____

EVENING REFLECTION

ONE MORE TIME, DESCRIBE YOUR PRIMARY EMOTION, THIS TIME WHAT IT HAS BEEN SINCE NOON.

☐ shame ☐ guilt ☐ excitement ☐ frustration

☐ anxiety ☐ joy ☐ fear ☐ boredom

☐ hope ☐ pride ☐ determination

TRY ONCE MORE TO DESCRIBE WHY.

_____

_____

_____

_____

WOULD JESUS WANT THIS TO BE YOUR PRIMARY EMOTION IN REGARD TO HIS HIGH CALL?

_____

_____

_____

_____

WHAT WOULD HE WANT IT TO BE?

_____

_____

_____

_____

_____

_____

END OF DAY FOCUS

Dwell on the emotion you believe Jesus primarily wants in you when it comes to His call on your life.

Imagine yourself filled with this emotion as you go to sleep.

DAY 5

MORNING QUOTE

"Jesus says to him, 'Follow me.' but the man replied, 'Lord, first let me go and bury my father.' Jesus said to Him, 'Let the dead bury their own dead, but you go and proclaim the kingdom of God.'"

— Luke 9:59-60

MORNING SUGGESTION

Complete your own answer.
LORD, I WILL FOLLOW YOU, BUT FIRST LET ME...

NOON REMINDER

"We treat our relationship with Jesus like the diet we keep meaning to start. I'm going to start eating right...as soon as I finish off this chicken chimichanga."

— Kyle Idleman, not a fan. Series

This seems like an appropriate quote for lunchtime!

WHAT ARE YOU PUTTING OFF THAT JESUS IS ASKING YOU TO DO TODAY?

_____

_____

_____

_____

WHAT DOES PUTTING THIS OFF DO FOR YOU?

_____

_____

_____

_____

_____

WHAT DOES PUTTING THIS OFF DO TO YOU?

_____

_____

_____

_____

_____

EVENING REFLECTION

Kyle mentioned the "As now, so then" principle. What I am today, unless I take decisive action, will be what I will be tomorrow.

IF AS YOU ARE NOW, YOU WILL ALWAYS BE, WHAT WILL YOU BE FOR THE REST OF YOUR LIFE?

_____

_____

_____

_____

_____

WHAT DO YOU THINK OF THIS DESCRIPTION?

_____

_____

_____

_____

_____

_____

_____

END OF DAY FOCUS

Imagine yourself as you hope to be someday.

DAY 6

MORNING QUOTE

"Jesus calls us to take up a cross and die. Not someday when we take our last physical breath, but to die to ourselves today...Bruce Thielemann is an author, he wrote these words, 'Please don't say anything to me about tomorrow. Tomorrow is a word the Bible does not know. The Holy Spirit's word is "today."'

The Bible says, 'Today, if you hear his voice, do not harden your hearts' (Hebrews 3:15). Today is the day of salvation. Don't say tomorrow. The word is 'today.'"

– Kyle Idleman, not a fan. Series

WHAT WILL YOU DO – WHAT WILL YOU BE – TODAY? PORTRAY IT IN WORDS BELOW.

NOON REMINDER

IT IS STILL TODAY. WHAT DO YOU FIND YOURSELF PUTTING OFF FOR TOMORROW THAT YOU ARE BEING CALLED TO TODAY?

EVENING REFLECTION

WHAT DO YOU WISH YOU HAD DONE, OR BEEN, OR SAID TODAY? I WISH I HAD...

_____

_____

_____

_____

_____

_____

_____

END OF DAY FOCUS

Today is over, never to return. But God is not stuck in today.

"...His compassions never fail. They are new every morning..."

— Lamentations 3:22-23

Go to sleep looking forward to meeting Jesus' compassion in the morning.

MORNING QUOTE

"...I will follow you, Lord; but first let me go back and say goodbye to my family.' Jesus replied, 'No one who puts his hand to the plow and looks back is fit for service in the kingdom of God.'"

— Luke 9:61-62

What is your "but first"? I will follow, but first let me... have some fun, build this house, get married, make a million dollars?

WHATEVER YOUR "BUT FIRST" IS, IMAGINE ENJOYING, ACCOMPLISHING, OR GAINING THAT. DESCRIBE WHAT THAT WOULD BE LIKE.

AT THAT TIME, WILL YOU REALLY BE ANY MORE LIKELY TO FULLY FOLLOW JESUS? WILL YOU BE LESS LIKELY?

NOON REMINDER

Bride: "Can we skip over the 'for richer or for poorer' section; I'm not ready to sign up for that."

Groom: "And can we cut the 'forsaking all others' bit? I don't want to tie myself down. I want to keep my options open."

WHAT HAVE YOU FOUND YOURSELF TEMPTED TO SAY TO JESUS TODAY?

LORD CAN WE JUST SKIP...

AND JESUS CAN WE JUST CUT OUT THE...

WHAT DOES HE REPLY?

EVENING REFLECTION

"When we try to follow Jesus without dying, we find ourselves frustrated with our failure and tired of trying. Following Jesus doesn't mean that you keep trying, it means that you keep dying."

– Kyle Idleman, not a fan. Series

HOW WOULD YOU PORTRAY THIS LAST WEEK FOR YOU, AS "TRYING" OR "DYING"?

WHICH WOULD BE EASIER - TRYING OR DYING?

WHICH DO YOU REALLY WANT TO DO?

END OF DAY FOCUS

Imagine your negative self, your old self, your selfish self, dying as you sleep; and a new self awaking, a Christ-filled, hope-saturated, love-centered person resurrecting with the new day.

not a fan.

WEEK FIVE

DEAD MEN'S BONES

WEEK FIVE

DEAD MEN'S BONES

WHAT STOOD OUT TO YOU FROM LESSON 5?

MORNING QUOTE

"Those people are where they are for a reason. You work hard, you live a good life, and you get ahead. There are rules in life. All the good intentions in the world can't change that."

– Bill, not a fan. Series

MORNING SUGGESTION

In the video, these words tumble out of Bill's mouth naturally. His words are what might be called Bill's worldview. It is how he sees life. It is how he believes the world works. A worldview is what automatically comes to mind when we are proving our point, defending ourselves, explaining things to our kids, and so on. In our minds, this is just the way it really is.

COMPLETE THE SENTENCES BELOW WITH YOUR AUTO-MATIC THOUGHTS NOT WHAT YOU WISHED YOU THOUGHT, BUT HOW YOU REALLY SEE LIFE.

People are... _____

The way to get ahead is... _____

The most important thing in life is... _____

I am... _____

When you mess up... _____

The way to be happy is... _____

God is... _____

NOON REMINDER

HOW DID YOU LIVE YOUR MORNING? WHAT RULES WERE MOST IMPORTANT?

_____

_____

_____

_____

_____

_____

_____

_____

EVENING REFLECTION

TRY TO PUT YOUR TRUE WORLDVIEW INTO WORDS AGAIN.

The purpose of life is... _____

The most important thing in life is... _____

What makes me who I am is... _____

Everyone ought to... _____

Jesus is... _____

WHEN IT COMES TO YOUR WORLDVIEW, WITH WHAT WOULD JESUS AGREE?

_____

_____

_____

_____

_____

_____

_____

_____

WITH WHAT WOULD HE DISAGREE?

_____

_____

_____

_____

_____

_____

_____

_____

_____

END OF DAY FOCUS

Go to sleep with the question in mind: Could I be wrong about some things I have long thought were totally true?

DAY 2

MORNING QUOTE

"Fans are very much caught up in an outward appearance. They think that somehow God is going to be impressed with their religious rule keeping or rituals or their traditions. There's nothing wrong with those things, in and of themselves. The problem comes when we do those things and it's not out of a pursuit of Jesus or a relationship with Him, but as a way to prove or measure our own spirituality."

— Kyle Idleman, not a fan. Series

MORNING REFLECTION

What are the primary "Christian" things you do? Prayer? Worship attendance? Morning quiet time? Working through this journal? Going to small group? List the "Christian" things you do in the left-hand column. In the right-hand column, list your primary motivation or reason for doing what you wrote on the left side.

Are you doing it because you should? To be a good example to others? To avoid guilt? To become a better person? Because others expect it? Because you always have? To know Jesus better? To avoid Hell?

"Christian" Things I Do	My Motivation

WHAT DO YOU LEARN FROM YOUR ANSWERS?

NOON REMINDER

WHY ARE YOU DOING THIS "NOON REMINDER"? SO YOU CAN FEEL GOOD THAT YOU COMPLETED EACH PAGE? SO YOU CAN TELL THE GROUP YOU DID IT? TO WARD OFF TEMPTATION? TO RECONNECT TO JESUS?

_____

_____

_____

_____

_____

Whatever your reason, imagine you are now spending this brief time because Jesus is so worthy, so loving, so desirous, that you just want to be filled with His presence all the more.

WHAT WOULD HAVING SUCH AN ATTITUDE BE LIKE FOR YOU?

_____

_____

_____

IF YOU REALLY WANTED TO KNOW JESUS, TO BE FILLED
WITH HIM, TO EXPERIENCE HIM, TO FULLY SEE HIM, WHAT
KINDS OF THINGS WOULD YOU DO TO MAKE THAT HAPPEN?
JOURNAL YOUR THOUGHTS.

END OF DAY FOCUS

WHICH OF THE THINGS YOU LISTED ABOVE COULD YOU DO
WHILE AWAITING SLEEP?

DAY 3

MORNING QUOTE

"It doesn't matter how accurate you are if you are aiming at the wrong goal."

— Kyle Idleman, not a fan. Series

MORNING SUGGESTION

WHAT GOAL WILL YOU AIM AT TODAY?
DESCRIBE YOUR GOAL BELOW.

_____

_____

_____

_____

_____

_____

_____

NOON REMINDER

THE GOAL YOU DESCRIBED THIS MORNING, WAS IT MORE ABOUT PASSIONATELY PURSUING JESUS? OR WAS IT MORE ABOUT BEING GOOD? OR MAYBE ABOUT AVOIDING BEING BAD? OR POSSIBLY JUST ABOUT SURVIVING?

How can you serve someone through social media today? What can you do to engage someone who seems sad? #iamnotafan

Finish this sentence:
MY GOAL FOR THE REST OF THIS DAY IS TO...

_____

_____

_____

_____

EVENING REFLECTION

WHAT DO YOU LIKE BEST ABOUT THE TIMES WHEN YOU PASSIONATELY PURSUE JESUS? TRY TO DESCRIBE WHAT YOU ENJOY MOST WHEN YOU ARE REALLY FOCUSED ON KNOWING AND LOVING JESUS.

_____

_____

_____

_____

_____

END OF DAY FOCUS

Go to sleep meditating on what it is like for you when you passionately pursue Jesus.

DAY 4

MORNING QUOTE

"You blind guides! You strain out a gnat but swallow a camel."

– Matthew 23:24

Straining out gnats is tedious, unrewarding work. If you swallow a gnat, you won't die. You won't even get sick. Gnats may look big and significant when they are floating in your soup, but in reality their presence is relatively inconsequential, especially when you have a camel lodged in your throat.

Ask the Holy Spirit to help you see the gnats at which you tend to strain - things which feel important to you but in actuality make very little difference in how well you know and love Jesus – in each of the areas below.

At church...
With my kids...
In my devotions...
When it comes to food, drink and clothes...
With my friends...

NOON REMINDER

HAVE YOU NOTICED ANY GNATS THIS MORNING, THINGS THAT FEEL REALLY IMPORTANT TO YOU BUT IN REALITY ARE FLEA-SIZED MATTERS IN A WORLD OF ELEPHANT-SIZED ISSUES? WRITE ABOUT THEM BELOW.

EVENING REFLECTION

Take a moment and imagine life without gnats, a life not straining over insignificant things that feel important but really aren't.

IN A SENTENCE, WHAT WOULD IT BE LIKE FOR YOU?

IF YOU COULD BE GNAT FREE, HOW WOULD IT AFFECT
OTHERS AND HOW THEY SEE YOU?

HOW WOULD JESUS LIKE IT?

_____

_____

_____

DECISION: FROM NOW ON, I WILL TREAT THE FOLLOWING AS GNATS RATHER THAN CAMELS...

_____

_____

_____

_____

_____

_____

END OF DAY FOCUS

Go to sleep meditating on a gnat-free life.

DAY 5

MORNING QUOTE

"Jesus explains the difference between these religious fans and true followers. And the fans are self-righteous and judgmental. They look down on others. But the followers of Jesus are humble and are quick to give the same grace to others that they've received from Jesus Christ."

– Kyle Idleman, not a fan. Series

MORNING SUGGESTION

WHICH WORDS BELOW BEST DESCRIBE YOU?

☐ humble   ☐ self-righteous   ☐ ashamed

☐ appreciative   ☐ judgmental   ☐ understanding

☐ angry   ☐ grieved   ☐ frustrated   ☐ serene

☐ sarcastic   ☐ encouraging

BASED ON YOUR ANSWERS, WOULD YOU SAY YOU ARE LIVING MORE UNDER:

( ) GRACE   ( ) LAW

The cure for pride isn't shame or self-loathing. The cure for pride is the humble act of receiving unconditional love. Sit with your hands open, your palms up, and imagine receiving undeserved, unconditional, unlimited love, forgiveness, grace and favor. Sit and receive the overflow of Heaven, a waterfall of unending grace, more than you can hold. Feel it flood your soul, fill your body like a glass full of cool water, filling you to the top of your head, and overflowing.

AFTER TAKING TIME TO IMAGINE THIS LOVE PERVADING YOU, GO BACK AND LOOK AT THE WORDS ABOVE AGAIN. WHAT, IF ANYTHING, CHANGES IN YOUR CHOICES?

NOON REMINDER

Sit before God, but this time with hands clinched and closed. Imagine yourself refusing unconditional love and grace. Imagine even shaking your fist, and saying to yourself, "I cannot be loved. I must earn everything I get. I will not take favors from anyone."

AS YOU DO, FEEL THE REACTION IN YOUR BODY. WHAT ARE YOUR SENSES TELLING YOU?

_____

_____

_____

_____

_____

_____

If you choose, gradually unclench your fists, open your hands, and ask for unconditional love. It will probably feel like a humbling act, even a child-like act. As you do, sense again the difference, what you are like, what life is like when you freely receive the unconditional love of Jesus.

EVENING REFLECTION

Again sit with your hands open. Finish these sentences in your mind. Journal your thoughts.

"I CAN'T RECEIVE UNCONDITIONAL LOVE BECAUSE..."

_____

_____

_____

_____

_____

_____

_____

"I MUST RECEIVE UNCONDITIONAL LOVE BECAUSE...."

_____

_____

_____

_____

_____

"WHAT DO YOU WANT TO PUT IN MY HANDS?"

END OF DAY FOCUS

Try going to sleep with your hands open.

DAY 6

MORNING QUOTE

"I walked away from God because I thought He was like you!"

– Eric, not a fan. Series

MORNING SUGGESTION

Answer the following questions.

IF PEOPLE THOUGHT JESUS WAS LIKE YOU, WHAT WOULD THEY LIKE ABOUT JESUS?

_____

_____

_____

_____

_____

_____

WHAT WOULDN'T THEY LIKE?

_____

_____

_____

_____

_____

_____

WOULD THEY WANT TO FOLLOW JESUS? WHY OR WHY NOT?

_____

_____

_____

_____

_____

_____

f ⃞ 🐦 What do you value most in other people? Use #iamnotafan and share with the Not a Fan community.

NOON REMINDER

WHAT QUALITY OF JESUS DO YOU MOST ADORE, MOST APPRECIATE?

_____

_____

_____

_____

_____

_____

EVENING REFLECTION

WHAT DIFFERENCE, IF ANY, DID REFLECTING ON A QUALITY OF JESUS YOU MOST APPRECIATE HAVE ON YOUR AFTER-NOON?

_____

_____

_____

_____

_____

WHAT WAS THIS EXPERIENCE LIKE?

_____

_____

_____

_____

_____

_____

_____

END OF DAY FOCUS

"Father, I have made you known to them, and will continue to make you known in order that the love you have for me may be in them and that I myself may be in them."

– John 17:26

MORNING QUOTE

"Come after" = a passionate pursuit

MORNING SUGGESTION

Journal about what would lead you, not just to pursue Jesus but, to pursue Him passionately. What would cause you to deeply desire to know Jesus, to move from rules to relationship?

_____

_____

_____

_____

_____

_____

NOON REMINDER

LIST FIVE THINGS YOU LOVE MOST, WHETHER IT IS ICE CREAM, SUNSETS, FLYING, CHILDREN, BASEBALL, WHATEVER!

1. _____

2. _____

3. _____

4. _____

5. _____

When an artist or inventor creates something, he puts some of himself into his creation. The creation reflects some aspect of the originator. Notice how Jesus is reflected in each of the things you listed.

For example, if you listed "children," in them you can see the playfulness and innocence of the One who created them. Or if you listed "the ocean," then you can sense the unfathomable depths, the great expanse, and the ever-changing-yet-always-the-sameness of the ocean's Creator.

LIST OUT HOW JESUS IS REFLECTED IN THE THINGS YOU LISTED.

1. _____

2. _____

3. _____

4. _____

5. _____

HOW DOES THIS EXERCISE AFFECT YOUR PASSION FOR JESUS?

_____

_____

_____

_____

_____

_____

_____

_____

EVENING REFLECTION

"We raised her in Church, but we didn't raise her in Christ."
— Distraught father to Kyle Idleman, not a fan. Series

Maybe you were raised in church but not in Christ. Now the choice is yours.

HOW WILL YOU LIVE YOUR LIFE, SIMPLY IN CHURCH, GOING THROUGH THE MOTIONS? OR IN CHRIST, PASSIONATELY PURSUING HIM? DESCRIBE YOUR THOUGHTS BELOW.

_____

_____

_____

_____

_____

_____

_____

END OF DAY FOCUS

Can you honestly say to Jesus as you prepare for sleep, "I love you. Above all, I love you and want to know you." If not, again think of your favorite things. See each of your favorite things flowing out of the playfulness, precision, fertility, profundity, power, wisdom and joy of Jesus Himself.

See how He is truly the King of Glory, and love Him.

WEEK SIX

DECISION TIME

WEEK SIX

DECISION TIME

WHAT STOOD OUT TO YOU FROM LESSON 6?

DAY 1

MORNING QUOTE

"I wish I could come over to your house and knock on your door. Hopefully, I could talk you into letting me come in and sit down for a few minutes. And I would want to sit across the kitchen table from you and look you in the eye and ask you this question...

Have you decided to follow Jesus?"

– Kyle Idleman, not a fan. Series

MORNING SUGGESTION

Rather than Kyle knocking on your door, imagine answering the bell, and it is Jesus Himself. He asks to come in. You offer him coffee or tea. He accepts. You sit down together, and He looks you in the eye, and asks in a voice full of compassion as well as authority: "Have you decided to follow me?"

JOURNAL YOUR RESPONSE BELOW.

_____

_____

_____

_____

_____

_____

_____

NOON REMINDER

Why do we have a "noon Reminder" in this journal? Because our decision to follow is not just daily; it is hourly; it is over and over and over.

ASK YOURSELF, "CAN I ACCEPT THE FACT THAT MY DECISION TO FOLLOW JESUS MUST BE MADE TIME AND TIME AGAIN, AND FOR THE REST OF MY LIFE?" WRITE YOUR THOUGHTS BELOW.

_____

_____

_____

_____

_____

_____

_____

_____

_____

EVENING REFLECTION

Remember the opening challenge of the series described in three letters: "DTR"? The initials stand for Define the Relationship. Maybe the question is now, "How have you redefined the relationship over the last several weeks?" Try to describe your redefined relationship with Jesus as it now stands using the questions below.

HOW DO YOU DEFINE THE RELATIONSHIP NOW?

_____

_____

_____

_____

_____

WHAT IS GOOD ABOUT IT?

_____

_____

_____

_____

_____

_____

_____

_____

WHAT STILL NEEDS WORK?

_____

_____

_____

_____

_____

_____

_____

_____

HOW WOULD JESUS DEFINE YOUR RELATIONSHIP?

END OF DAY FOCUS

A relationship is not like a rock - never changing, always the same. A relationship is more like a stream, always flowing, never quite identical moment to moment, either deepening or growing more shallow, widening or narrowing, if only little by little.

As you enter sleep, imagine your relationship with Jesus widening and deepening, and always changing for the rest of your life and into eternity.

DAY 2

MORNING QUOTE

"I was traveling down the I-75, fully convinced that I'm on the I-71, because the roads feel very much the same. Now in hindsight, I should have seen some signs. I'm sure there were some very clear markers that I was on the wrong road. But, I was so sure of myself, I never allowed for the possibility that I was going in the wrong direction."

— Kyle Idleman, not a fan. Series

MORNING SUGGESTION

DOES YOUR MIND EVEN ALLOW FOR THE POSSIBILITY THAT YOU MIGHT NOT BE A FOLLOWER OF JESUS?

I CAN'T FACE THE IDEA THAT I MIGHT NOT BE A FULLY DEVOTED FOLLOWER OF JESUS BECAUSE...

I AM FULLY WILLING TO CONSIDER THE FACT THAT I MIGHT NOT BE A TRUE FOLLOWER OF JESUS BECAUSE...

NOON REMINDER

"Enter through the narrow gate. For wide is the gate and broad is the road that leads to destruction, and many enter through it. But small is the gate and narrow the road that leads to life, and only a few find it."

— Matthew 7:13-14

READ THE PASSAGE THREE TIMES. UNDERLINE THE PHRASE THAT STANDS OUT TO YOU MOST. WRITE WHY THIS PHRASE STANDS OUT.

_____

_____

_____

_____

_____

EVENING REFLECTION

Kyle missed the signs that he was on I-75 rather than I-71.

WHAT ARE EACH OF THESE FOLLOWING "SIGNS" SAYING ABOUT YOU, AND WHETHER OR NOT YOU ARE A FOLLOWER OF JESUS?

YOUR CONSCIENCE.

YOUR FRIENDS.

YOUR FAMILY.

YOUR MENTOR.

YOUR LIFESTYLE.

_____

_____

_____

THE HOLY SPIRIT.

_____

_____

_____

END OF DAY FOCUS

"I'm just asking: what if many of us are traveling down what we think is the narrow road that leads to life, but we're actually on the broad road that leads to destruction? What if we have hit the cruise control and are traveling through life singing along to Christian radio with a Jesus fish on the bumper, completely unaware that we are headed to destruction? I'm not trying to make you paranoid or fearful. I believe that nothing can separate us from the love of God and my confidence is in Him who can keep me from falling. But clearly the Bible teaches that there are those who have a false assurance of salvation.

So, what if one day Jesus returns, and all kinds of good

church-going folks find out that, in the end, they were never on the right road? I'm just asking, is it possible that you think you're a follower, but you're really just a fan?

I don't want to make people unnecessarily question where they will spend eternity, but how can you read Matthew 7:13-14 without raising the question?"

AS YOU READ THE ABOVE PARAGRAPH, WAS YOUR HEART AT PEACE OR TROUBLED?

_____

_____

_____

_____

_____

_____

_____

Sit back, close your eyes: Imagine your To-Do list was done for the day. What is the very next thing you would do today? Use #iamnotafan and share with the Not a Fan community.

DAY 3

MORNING QUOTE

"Not everyone who says to me, 'Lord, Lord,' will enter the Kingdom of Heaven, but only he who does the will of my Father who is in heaven. Many will say to me on that day, 'Lord, Lord, did we not prophesy in your name, and in your name drive out demons and perform many miracles?' Then I will tell them plainly, 'I never knew you. Away from me, you evildoers!'"

— Matthew 7:21-23

"Jesus doesn't say this will happen to a few. He doesn't say some. He says many."

— Kyle Idleman, not a fan. Series

Kyle asks two big questions in the episode. Try to answer for yourself.

HAVE I DETERMINED THAT I AM A FOLLOWER BECAUSE I SAY I AM A FOLLOWER, OR IS IT BECAUSE I ACT LIKE A FOLLOWER?

HAVE I DETERMINED THAT I AM A FOLLOWER BASED ON RELIGIOUS MEASUREMENTS RATHER THAN LOVING DEEDS?

NOON REMINDER

I BELIEVE I AM A FOLLOWER OF JESUS BECAUSE...

_____

_____

_____

_____

_____

_____

EVENING REFLECTION

TODAY, COULD YOU BE CALLED AN "EVILDOER"? WHY OR WHY NOT?

_____

_____

_____

_____

_____

END OF DAY FOCUS

Has answering today's tough questions drawn you closer to Jesus or led you further away? Use today's final moments trying to discern why.

DAY 4

MORNING QUOTE

Eric: *"You don't need to be here. Go home."*
Natalie: *"Why? Just because I don't know her name?"*
Eric: *"Because you don't want to."*

MORNING SUGGESTION

Whose names don't you want to know? Think of the people in your life. Which person's name don't you care about?

MAKE A LIST, EVEN IF IT MUST BE BY DESCRIPTION IN THE CASES WHERE YOU REALLY DON'T KNOW THE PERSON'S NAME.

WHAT SIMILARITIES DO YOU SEE IN THESE PEOPLE THAT WOULD LEAD THEM TO BE PEOPLE WHOSE NAMES YOU DON'T WANT TO KNOW?

NOON REMINDER

WHOSE NAMES HAVE YOU WANTED, AND NOT WANTED TO KNOW, IN YOUR INTERACTIONS SO FAR TODAY? MAKE TWO LISTS, THEN DESCRIBE WHY.

Wanted	Not Wanted

EVENING REFLECTION

ARE YOU A FOLLOWER OF JESUS BASED ON THIS PARAGRAPH?

"One of the clues you may be more fan than follower is that when I asked 'Are you a follower' your mind immediately went to the fact that you come to church, put some money in the plate, volunteer from time to time. Let me just ask you a really blunt question: do you think God needs your help?

"Do you think you're earning His gratitude by ticking off a list of religious busywork? No, I'm not saying that attending church or giving money or reading your Bible are bad things to do. But think for a second. Why would those things matter to God? I believe they only matter to God as an expression of your closeness to Him. He doesn't need your help, you aren't going to impress Him, but He does long for you to be close to Him, for you to know Him intimately. And really, that's the question, isn't it? Do you know Jesus? Does He know you? That's what it comes down to. Does He have your heart? Is He your everything? Do you invest more in your relationship with Him than any other relationship? I think we sometimes confuse knowing about Jesus with knowing Jesus. But there is a difference between knowledge and intimacy."

— Kyle Idleman, not a fan. Series

END OF DAY FOCUS

Ask Jesus what matters to Him as you complete your day.

DAY 5

MORNING QUOTE

"If I speak in the tongues of men or of angels, but do not have love, I am only a resounding gong or a clanging cymbal. If I have the gift of prophecy and can fathom all mysteries and all knowledge, and if I have a faith that can move mountains, but do not have love, I am nothing. If I give all I possess to the poor and give over my body to hardship that I may boast, but do not have love, I gain nothing."

— 1 Corinthians 13:1-3

 **If you could give up your life as you know it, what would you do? Travel through Africa? Fight poverty and homelessness in the U.S.? Volunteer to help build schools in Nepal? Invent something to change the world? Share with us and inspire others by using** #iamnotafan **in your response.**

MORNING REFLECTION

THINK ABOUT THIS QUESTION CAREFULLY: WHEN DO YOU LOVE OTHERS THE BEST?

_____   When I focus on trying to manufacture unconditional love for others.

_____   When I focus on receiving the unconditional love of Jesus for me.

WHAT DO YOU LEARN FROM YOUR ANSWER?

_____

_____

_____

_____

_____

_____

NOON REMINDER

To follow Jesus is to love. Imagine Jesus encountering those you will likely encounter today.

WRITE OUT HOW HE WOULD LOOK AT THEM, WHAT HE WOULD SEE, HOW HE WOULD ACT TOWARD THEM.

EVENING REFLECTION

WOULD YOU SAY YOU HAVE BEEN A POSER TODAY OR THE REAL DEAL? JOURNAL YOUR RESPONSE.

_____

_____

_____

_____

_____

END OF DAY FOCUS

CONSIDER THE QUESTION: IS JESUS A POSER? DOES HE JUST PRETEND TO LOVE PEOPLE OR DOES HE REALLY LOVE THEM? WHAT DOES YOUR ANSWER MEAN TO YOU?

_____

_____

_____

_____

_____

_____

_____

_____

_____

DAY 6

MORNING QUOTE

"Jesus is not impressed because His name is on your bumper sticker, or because you have Christian music on your iPod, or because you never miss a weekend at church, or you give to all the right causes. And those things are all good, but they are only good to the extent that they are done out of love for Him. Jesus says that He wants us to love Him with all of our heart and soul and mind and strength. And then He says, 'Love your neighbor as yourself.' It is love that reveals us to be real followers of Jesus Christ...Jesus wants you to love Him enough to take up your cross. So for you, which is it? What road have you chosen? Fan, or Follower? It all comes down to love."

– Kyle Idleman, not a fan. Series

Imagine putting love at the top of your to-do list today. Imagine yourself encouraging the various people you will likely see, and overflowing with love, concern, care.

JOT SOME NOTES ON WHAT IT WOULD BE LIKE, HOW IT WOULD BE DIFFERENT FROM OTHER DAYS.

NOON REMINDER

WHO IS THE MOST LOVING PERSON YOU KNOW? YOUR GRANDMOTHER? YOUR SPOUSE? A COLLEGE FRIEND? DESCRIBE THAT PERSON BELOW.

EVENING REFLECTION

Imagine someone you know answering the question from today's noon reminder with your name.

WHAT WOULD YOU WANT THEM TO WRITE? HOW WOULD YOU LIKE ANOTHER TO DESCRIBE YOU?

_____

_____

_____

_____

_____

END OF DAY FOCUS

Close your day praying prayers of love for those you care about.

DAY 7

 **If you could do just one thing today what would it be? Use #iamnotafan and share with the Not a Fan community.**

MORNING QUOTE

"'Lord, please help me. Because I know that without You, I can do nothing. And I know that without love I am nothing. Without love, it doesn't matter what I say. It doesn't matter how much faith I have. It doesn't matter how much I give. The only way I can be anything is if I am Yours and the only way people will know that I am Yours is if I love.' That was my father. It still is."

– Natalie reading from her dad's journal, not a fan. Journal

IMAGINE SOMEONE FINDING AND READING THIS JOURNAL OF YOURS. HOW WOULD YOU FEEL ABOUT IT?

IF YOUR FOCUS WAS ON "SELF" YOU MIGHT BE EMBAR-
RASSED OR POSSIBLY PROUD. IF YOUR FOCUS WAS ON
JESUS, HOW WOULD YOU FEEL?

NOON REMINDER

WHO COMES TO MIND FROM YOUR STUDY GROUP? WRITE
A PRAYER FOR HIM OR HER.

EVENING REFLECTION

WHAT KINDS OF THINGS DO YOU WISH YOU HAD WRITTEN IN THIS JOURNAL?

_____

_____

_____

_____

This is your last entry in the *not a fan. Journal*.

WHAT PRACTICES DO YOU SEE YOURSELF INCLUDING IN YOUR LIFE IN ORDER TO BEST CONTINUE TO BUILD YOUR RELATIONSHIP WITH JESUS AS HIS FOLLOWER?

_____

_____

_____

_____

_____

_____

_____

_____

_____

_____

_____

_____

_____

_____

_____

_____

END OF DAY FOCUS

Try softly singing or humming these words as you enter sleep:

I have decided to follow Jesus.
I have decided to follow Jesus.
I have decided to follow Jesus.
No turning back, no turning back.

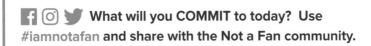 **What will you COMMIT to today? Use #iamnotafan and share with the Not a Fan community.**